CLAY CHARM
Magic!

CLAY CHARM
Magic!

25 Amazing, Teeny-Tiny Projects to Make with Polymer Clay

Helga Jiang

Sky Pony Press
New York

All Rights Reserved. No part of this book may be reproduced in any manner without the express written consent of the publisher, except in the case of brief excerpts in critical reviews or articles. All inquiries should be addressed to Sky Pony Press, 307 West 36th Street, 11th Floor, New York, NY 10018.

Sky Pony Press books may be purchased in bulk at special discounts for sales promotion, corporate gifts, fund-raising, or educational purposes. Special editions can also be created to specifications. For details, contact the Special Sales Department, Skyhorse Publishing, 307 West 36th Street, 11th Floor, New York, NY 10018 or info@skyhorsepublishing.com.

Sky Pony® is a registered trademark of Skyhorse Publishing, Inc. ®, a Delaware corporation.

www.skyhorsepublishing.com

10 9 8 7 6 5 4 3 2 1

Manufactured in China, June 2014
This product conforms to CPSIA 2008

Library of Congress Cataloging-in-Publication Data is available on file.

Cover designed by Owen Corrigan
Large cover photo by Thinkstock
Small cover photos by Helga Jiang

Print ISBN: 978-1-63220-398-4
Ebook ISBN: 978-1-63220-399-1

CONTENTS

LiST OF TOOLS:

1. Polymer Clay
2. Dotting Tools
3. Varnish/Gloss Finish
4. Paintbrush
5. Toothpicks
6. Cookie Cutter
7. Eye Pins
8. Needle Tool
9. Blade
10. Chalk Pastels
11. Liquid Clay
12. Bottle Cap
13. Rolling Pin/Cylindrical Tool
14. Acrylic Paint

FAUX-KNIT PATTERN

These adorable knitted hearts can make anyone feel
warm and cozy inside. Use this simple technique for
miniature sweaters or braids!

Instructions:

1. Using a rolling pin, flatten a sheet of clay. This will be the base for your pattern.

2. Roll out two strands of clay. Roll the clay back and forth against a clean, flat surface to create long strands.

3. Twist these strands together.

4. Repeat steps 1–2, but twist in the opposite direction. You will be left with a pair of twisted ropes.

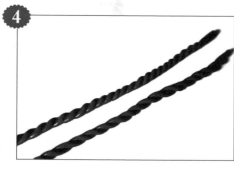

5. Join these two ropes and voila! You can stop here if you're making a braid.

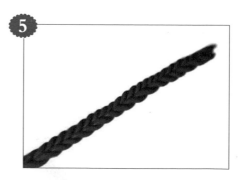

6. Create more of these and join them together on top of your base until you have your desired width.

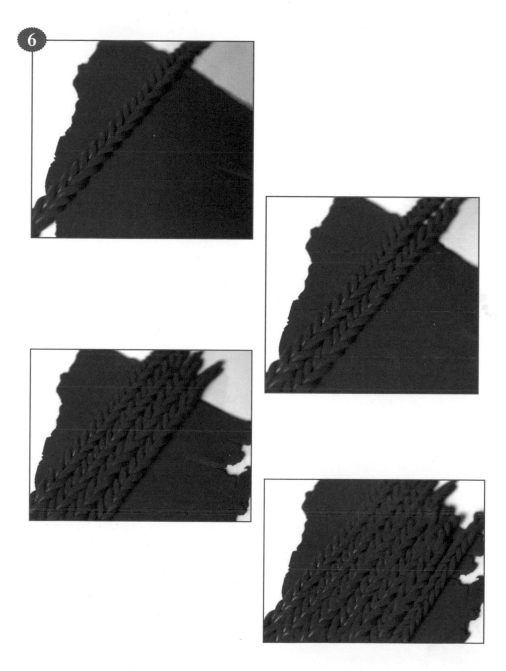

7. Use a cookie cutter to cut out a shape of your choice. You can also cut out a shape yourself using a blade, but be careful!

8. Stick an eye pin on top to turn your shape into a charm.

9. Bake using the instructions on your clay package.

TEDDY BEAR

Difficulty Level: **Easy**

Materials:

Polymer Clay (Tan, Dark Brown) • Dotting tool • Needle Tool • Eye Pin • Paintbrush, Varnish (Optional)

This cute teddy bear is perfect for the smallest of snuggles. Wear him as a bracelet, a cell phone charm, or keep him close to your heart on a necklace.

Instructions:

1. Roll out two spheres and place them on top of one another.

2. Add the feet and paws.

3. Add the ears and the
   snout.

4. Use a dotting tool to
   indent details on the ears
   and feet.

5. Using a darker brown color, add the eyes and
   nose.

6. Using a needle tool, make stitch markings. Now it looks like a real teddy bear!

7. Insert an eye pin.

8. Bake using the instructions on your clay package.

9. (Optional) Let the charm cool completely before glazing the eyes and nose with varnish for a glossy shine.

BLUeBeRRY PiE

This traditional dessert fave is a mouthwatering mini.

Instructions:

1. Flatten ecru-colored clay.

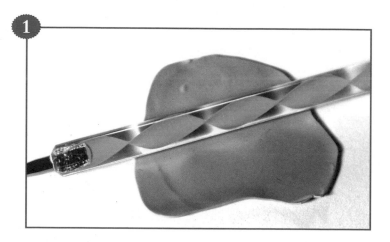

2. Spread this sheet
   of clay onto a
   bottle cap.

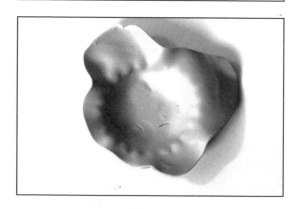

3. Press the clay against the cap. Cut off any excess clay with a blade. Be careful!

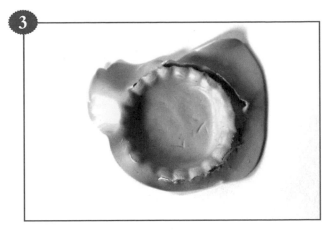

4. Fill the pie halfway with clay.

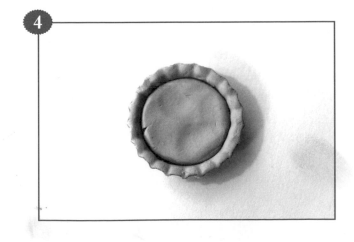

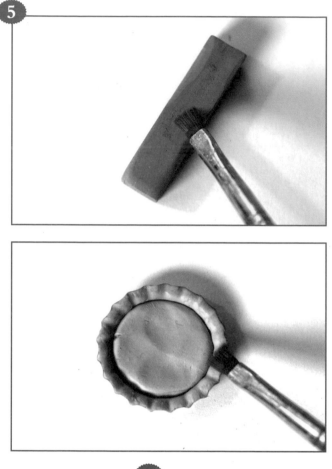

5. Use a brush with orange chalk pastels to shade the pie crust. This will give it a baked look.

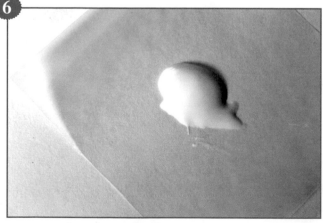

6. Place liquid clay onto a separate area.

7. Using a blade, scrape off some blue and purple chalk pastels and mix into the liquid clay with a toothpick.

8. Take tiny pieces of blue clay and roll each in circular motions to create spheres for the blueberries. Mix them with the liquid.

9. Spread the blueberries onto the pie.

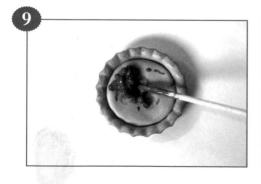

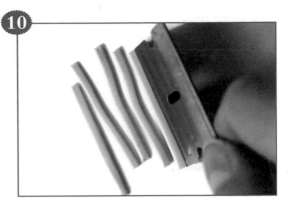

10. Cut out six thin strips of ecru colored clay.

11. Create a lattice top for the pie.

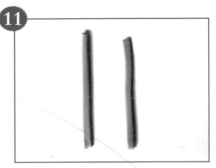

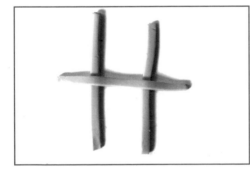

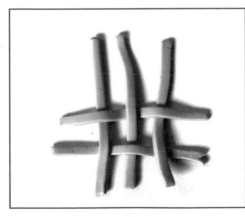

12. Shade the clay
with orange
chalk pastels, like
in step 5.

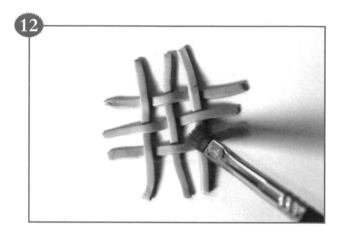

13. Apply the lattice
top to the pie
and cut off any
excess.

14. Bake your piece using the instructions on your clay package. Let cool completely before glazing the blueberries with varnish.

STRAWBERRY JAM-FILLED COOKIES

These are perfect for a clay tea party. Show your best friends how much you love them by giving them these heart-shaped confections, or show them how to make them on their own!

Instructions:

1. Flatten ecru-colored clay using a rolling pin.

2. Using a cookie cutter, cut out two of the same shape.

3. Use the bristles of a toothbrush to texture the cookie.

4. Use orange chalk–pastels to dust the cookie. This will give the cookie a baked look.

5. In one of the cookies, cut out a heart shape. You may use another cookie cutter or you can cut a shape out yourself using a blade. Be careful!

6. Mix liquid clay and red chalk pastels to create the jam filling.

7. Spread the filling onto the center of the plain cookie.

8. Stick an eye pin on top to make it a charm.

9. Take the non-jam cookie and place it on top of the other. You'll be able to see the jam through the shape you cut. Use a toothpick to clean up the jam.

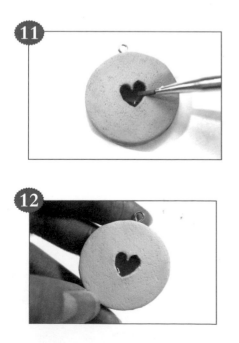

10. Bake using the instructions on your clay package.

11. Let the charm cool completely. Glaze the jam center with a paintbrush dipped in varnish to give it a beautiful shine.

12. Let the varnish dry completely before handling.

CHOCOLATE CHIP COOKIE

Difficulty Level: **Easy**

Materials:

Polymer Clay (Ecru, Dark Brown) • Chalk Pastels (Orange) •
Tin Foil • Toothbrush • Eye Pin • Paintbrush • Varnish

Add to your clay charm dessert collection with a batch
of fresh chocolate chip cookies. You'll be tempted to grab
one while they're still hot!

Instructions:

1. Start by flattening a sphere of ecru-colored clay.

2. Take some tin foil and scrunch it up.

3. Press the foil against the clay. This will help add a cookie-like texture.

4. Using the bristles of a toothbrush, give the cookie more texture.

5. Brush orange chalk pastels around the perimeter of the cookie. This will give it a baked effect.

6. Roll a strand of dark brown clay. Cut off chocolate chips and add them to the cookie.

7. Insert an eye pin.

8. Bake the charm using the instructions on your clay package.

9. Let the charm cool completely before glazing the chocolate chips with varnish.

DOUBLE CHEESEBURGER

Difficulty Level: **Medium**

Materials:

Polymer Clay (Tan, Brown, Yellow) • Chalk Pastels (Orange, Brown) • Dotting Tool • Toothpick • Rolling Pin • Blade • Eye Pin • Paintbrush • Varnish

Not satisfied with double trouble? Add as many ingredients as you want on this tiny burger.

Instructions:

1. Flatten two spheres of tan clay. One should be larger than the other.

2. Use orange and brown chalk pastels to dust the clay.

3. Using a toothpick, make tiny circular motions to texture the base of the buns.

4. Flatten two spheres of brown clay for the meat. Use a dotting tool to texture the edges of the meat.

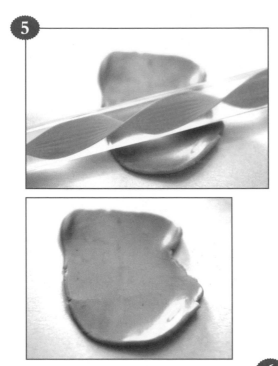

5. Using a rolling pin or cylindrical tool, flatten a sheet of yellow clay.

6. Use a blade to cut out two squares.

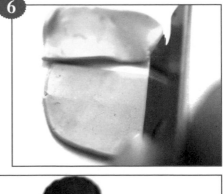

7. Stack the ingredients.
   Make your burgers as tall
   and tasty as you want.

8. Insert an eye pin.

9. Using the instructions on your clay package, bake the charm.

10. Let the charm cool completely before glazing the charm with varnish for a glossy shine.

BLUEBERRY MUFFIN

Do you know the muffin man, the muffin man, the muffin man? Do you know the muffin man who lives on Clay Charm Lane!

Instructions:

1. Start by creating the base of the muffin. With a sphere of ecru-colored clay, use your fingers to mold a cupcake-like shape.

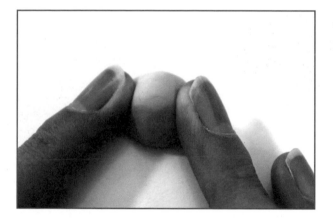

2. Use a toothpick to make indents along the edge.

3. With the bristles of a toothbrush, texture the clay.

4. Create a hemisphere with the same colored clay for the muffin top.

5. Join the two parts.

6. Texture the top with a toothbrush (see step 3).

7. Dust the clay using orange chalk pastels to give the muffin a baked look.

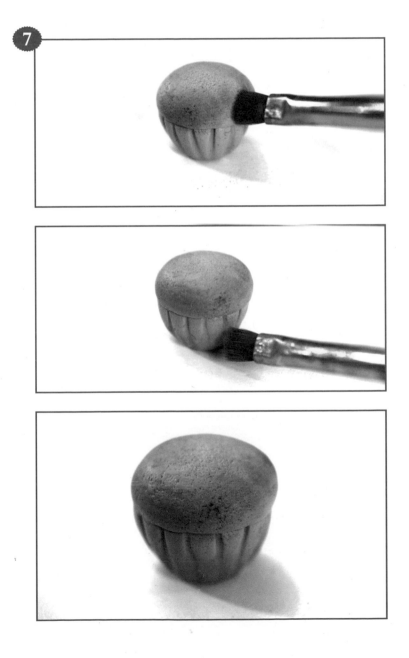

8. Take blue clay and roll into tiny pieces to make the blueberries.
   Push the tiny pieces of blue clay into the muffin with a toothpick.

9. Insert an eye pin.

10. Using the instructions on your clay package, bake the charm.

11. After the charm has cooled completely, glaze the blueberries with varnish for a brilliant shine.

THREE PEAS IN A POD

Difficulty Level: **Easy**

Materials:

Polymer Clay (Light Green, Dark Green) • Rolling Pin • Acrylic Paint (Black, Pink) • Dotting Tool • Eye Pin • Toothpick • Paintbrush • Varnish

You'll be happy as these little peas when you've created this charm.

Instructions:

1. Roll out three, same-sized spheres of light green clay.

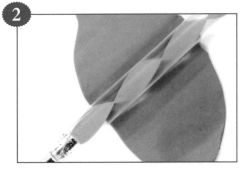

2. With a rolling pin or cylindrical tool, flatten a sheet of dark green clay.

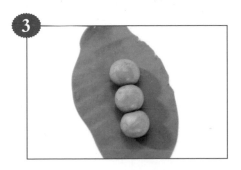

3. Place the three peas on top.

4. Cut out a rectangle around the peas.

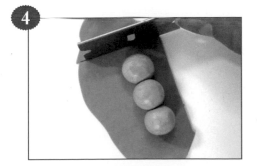

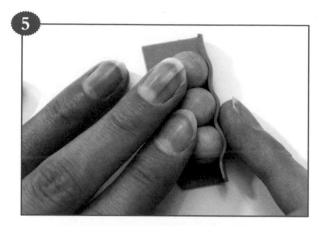

5. Fold the dark green sheet toward the peas on either side.

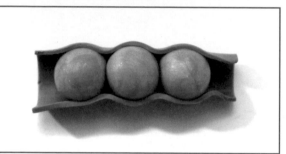

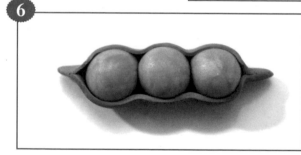

6. Pinch the ends.

7. Insert an eye pin.

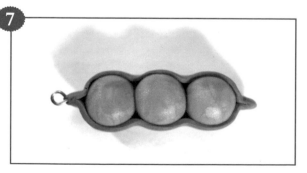

8. Bake the charm, following the instructions on your clay package.

9. Let the charm cool completely.

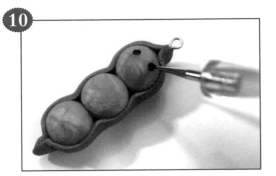

10. Dip a dotting tool in black acrylic paint and dot on the eyes.

11. Use a toothpick to draw on a winking face.

12. Use pink acrylic paint for the blush.

13. Let the paint dry completely.

14. Glaze the charm with a coat of varnish to set the paint and give a brilliant shine.

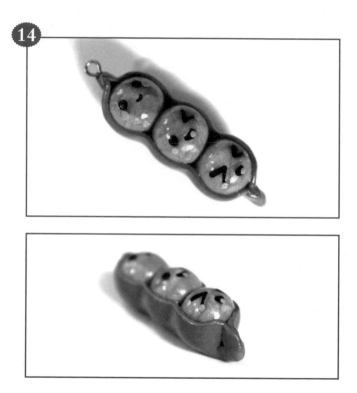

SKUNK

Fortunately for you, this guy has all of the cuteness
without any of the stinkiness!

Instructions:

1. Start with an oval-shaped ball of black clay.

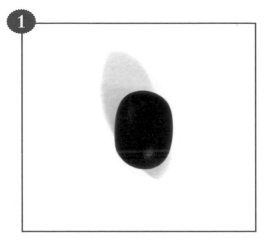

2. Pinch the top to create a nose.

3. Sculpt the tail.

4. Add the tail to the back of the skunk.

5. Slightly curl the tip of the tail.

6. Add two small spheres of clay for the ears.

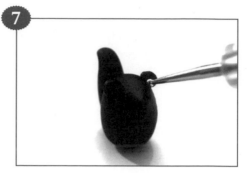

7. Using a dotting tool, indent the ears.

8. Insert an eye pin.

9. Bake using the instructions on your clay package.

10. Let the charm cool completely before painting on the details.

11. With a dotting tool dipped in white paint, dot on the whites of the eyes.

12. With a toothpick dipped in black paint, dot on the pupils.

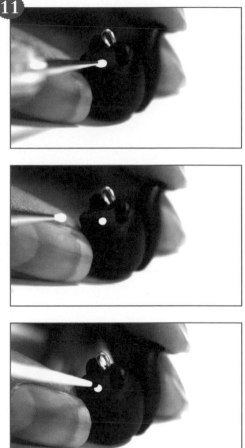

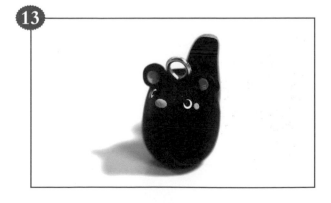

13. Use pink paint for the blush, ears, and nose.

14. Use a toothpick to draw on the white on the tail, back, and belly.

15. Let the paint dry completely.

16. With a paintbrush dipped in varnish, glaze the charm to set the paint and give a brilliant shine.

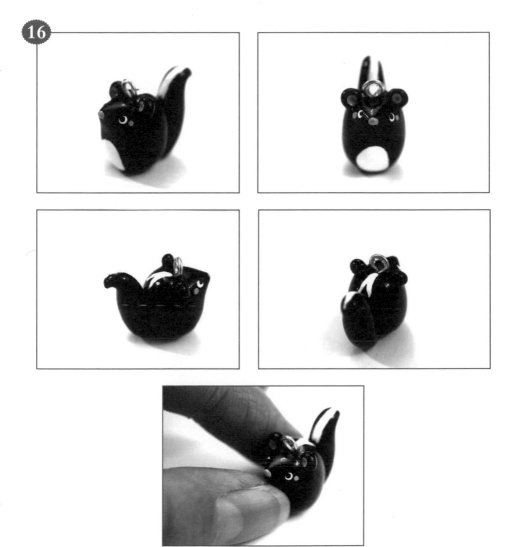

MAGICIAN'S RABBIT HAT

Difficulty Level: **Medium**

Materials:

Polymer Clay (Black, White, Pink) • Dotting Tool •
Eye Pin • Paintbrush • Varnish

Impress your friends by creating a little clay magic of your own. This goofy rabbit hat is a great alternative to a card trick.

Instructions:

1. Roll out a cylinder of black clay. This will be the base of the hat.

2. Add a flat circle to the top.

3. Roll a small circle of white clay and place it on top of the flat circle, making the head of the rabbit.

4. Add the ears and paws.

5. Insert an eye pin.

6. Use black clay for the eyes.

7. Add pink clay for the blush and ears.

8. Use a dotting tool to push the pink clay into the ears.

9. Using the instructions on your clay package, bake the charm.

10. Let the charm cool completely before glazing with varnish for a glossy shine.

PANDA

Difficulty Level: **Easy**

Materials:

Polymer Clay (Black, White, Pink, Red) • Eye Pin • Paintbrush • Varnish

Just like the teddy bear, the panda is the perfect clay charm companion. Make sure you have some bamboo nearby!

Instructions:

1. Place two white spheres on top of one another.

2. Add on the feet, paws, and ears.

3. Add flattened black clay for the eyes.

4. Add small white circles.

5. Use pink clay for the blush.

6. Don't forget the tail!

7. (Optional) Add on a red heart for the panda to hold!

8. Insert an eye pin.

9. Follow the baking instructions on your clay package.

10. Let the charm cool completely before glazing with varnish for a glossy shine.

PEANUT BUTTER & JELLY FRIENDSHIP CHARMS

Difficulty Level: **Easy**

Materials:

Polymer Clay (Ecru, Tan) • Rolling Pin • Toothpick • Chalk
Pastels (Brown, Orange, Purple) • Blade • Liquid Clay •
Eye Pin • Paintbrush • Varnish

Instead of ordinary friendship bracelets, give your BFF
something special with these amazing sandwich charms.

Instructions:

1. Flatten a sheet of ecru-colored clay.

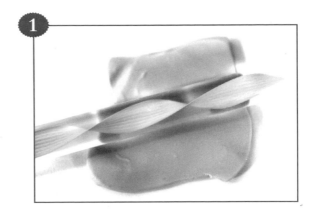

2. Cut out a square.

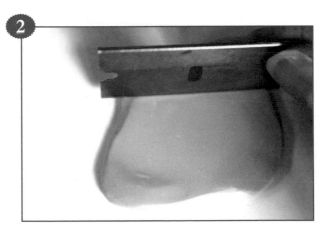

3. Round the corners.

4. Texture the clay
   with the bristles of
   a toothbrush.

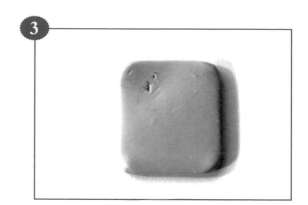

5. Indent the sides with a
   toothpick.

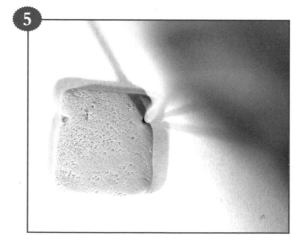

6. Dust the edges using brown chalk pastels and a brush.

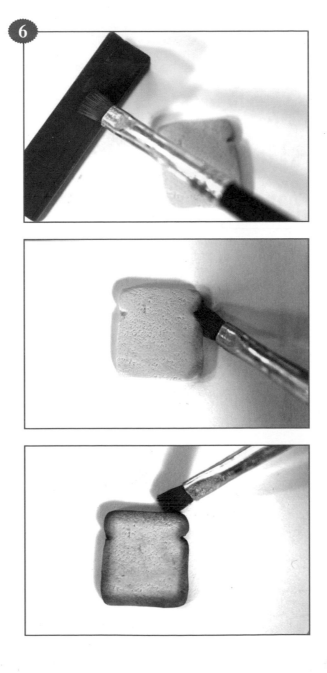

7. Dust the center of the bread with orange chalk pastels.

8. Insert an eye pin.

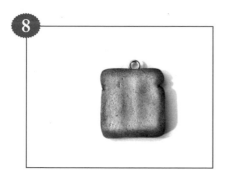

9. Repeat steps 1–8 to create a second slice of bread.

10. Mix purple chalk pastels and liquid clay for the jam.

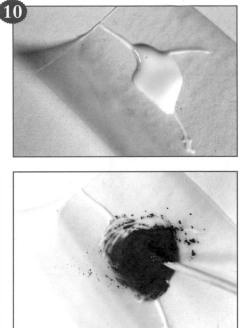

11. Spread the jam on one of the slices.

12. For the peanut butter, mix small pieces of tan clay and liquid clay.

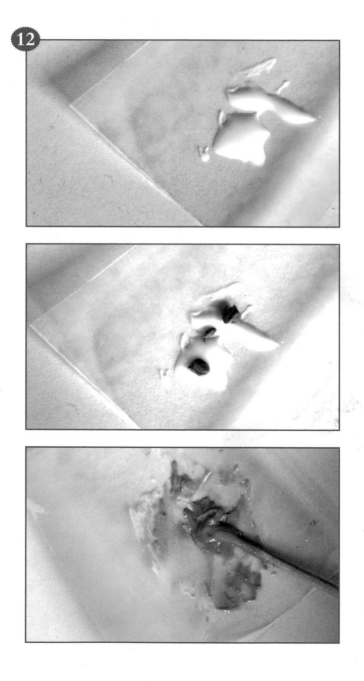

13. Spread the peanut butter on the remaining slice.

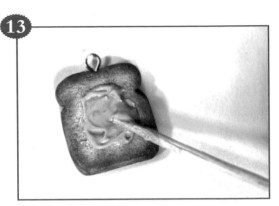

14. Bake your charms by following the instructions on your clay package. Add varnish to the jelly and peanut butter to give a nice shine.

STRAWBERRY SHORTCAKE

Difficulty Level: **Medium**

Materials:

Polymer Clay (Ecru, White, Red) • Needle Tool or
Toothpick • Eye Pin • Paintbrush • Varnish

Have your cake and eat it too with this fluffy shortcake
charm. Delicious!

Instructions:

1. Flatten two ecru-colored spheres of the same size.

2. Place white clay in between.

3. With a needle tool (or toothpick), use tiny circular motions to create a crumby, cake texture.

4. Add a small white swirl to the top.

5. Add small pieces of red clay for the strawberries.

6. Insert an eye pin.

7. Bake using the instructions on your clay package.

8. Glaze the cream and strawberries with varnish.

S'MORES

Difficulty Level: **Easy**

Materials:

Polymer Clay (Ecru, White, Brown) • Chalk Pastels (Orange)
• Paintbrush • Toothpick • Toothbrush • Eye Pin • Varnish

Take these s'mores on your next camping trip. They're
bound to be a hit around the campfire.

Instructions:

1. Cut out a square of ecru-colored clay.

2. Use a toothpick to indent the center.

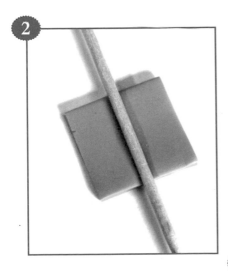

3. Add texture with the bristles of a toothbrush.

4. Poke patterned holes into the cracker.

5. Repeat steps 1-4 to create a second graham cracker.

6. Dust the crackers with orange chalk pastels to give them a baked effect.

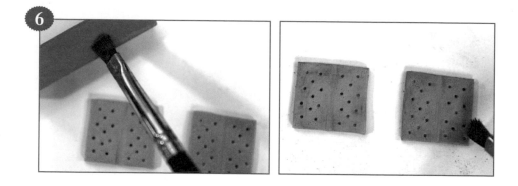

7. Create the chocolate and marshmallow as shown.

8. Stack the ingredients!

9. Insert an eye pin.

10. Bake using the instructions on your clay package.

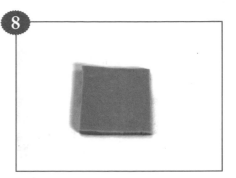

11. Let the charm cool completely before glazing the chocolate and marshmallow with varnish.

FOX

Difficulty Level: **Medium**

Materials:

Polymer Clay (Orange) • Dotting Tool • Paintbrush • Acrylic
Paint (White, Black, Pink) • Varnish • Eye Pin

The cleverest of all clay charms, the wily fox is always
happy to keep you company.

Instructions:

1. Start with a ball of orange clay for the body.

2. Add a pointed head.

3. Attach triangular ears.

4. Indent the ears with a dotting tool.

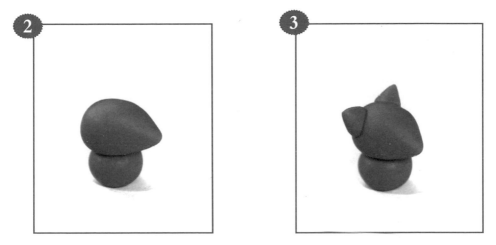

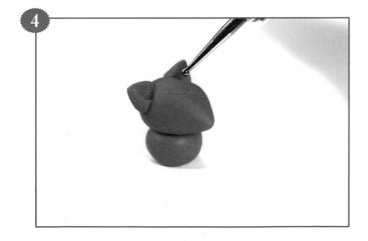

5. Add the tail.

6. Insert an eye pin.

7. Bake the charm using the instructions on your clay package.

8. Let the charm cool completely.

9. Paint the facial features using toothpicks and paintbrushes dipped in acrylic paint.

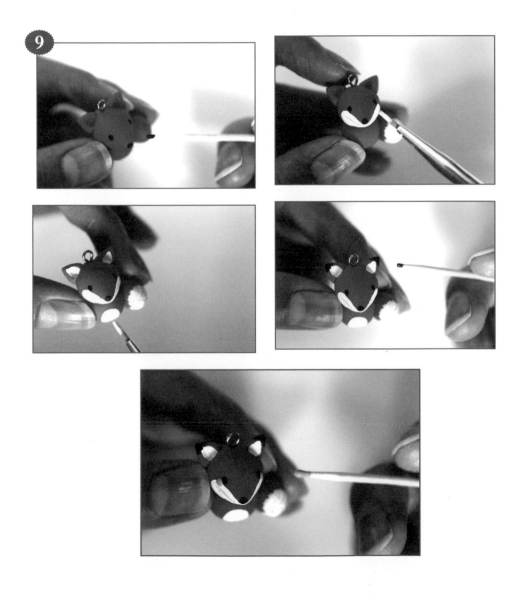

10. Let the paint dry completely before glazing the charm with varnish for a glossy shine.

DONUTS

Better than Dunk'n! These hot and sweet donuts
are ideal at breakfast.

Instructions:

1. Slightly flatten a ball of ecru-colored clay.

2. Poke a hole in the center of the circle with a dotting tool.

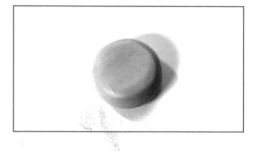

3. Create the icing by mixing liquid clay and pieces of solid clay (color of your choice). Spread this on your donut.

4. (Optional) Decorate the donut with embellishments. You may use micro-beads (as shown) or create your own with clay.

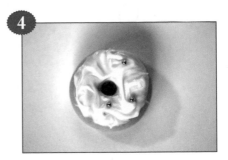

5. Insert an eye pin.

6. Bake the donuts using the instructions on your clay package.

CAT

Difficulty Level: **Easy**

Materials:

Polymer Clay (Gray, Black, Pink) • Dotting Tool • Paintbrush • Varnish • Eye Pin

What's cuter than a kitten? A teeny, tiny clay kitten charm!

Instructions:

1. Stack two balls of gray clay on top of one another.

2. Attach triangular ears.

3. Add a tail.

4. Using a dotting tool, indent the ears.

5. Add the eyes and nose with black clay.

6. Roll out thin strands of black clay for the whiskers.

7. Add pink clay for the blush and belly.

8. Insert an eye pin.

9. Bake using the instructions on your clay package.

10. Glaze the charm with varnish for a glossy shine.

RED VELVET CUPCAKE

Difficulty Level: **Medium**

Materials:

Polymer Clay (Red, White) • Liquid Clay • Needle Tool or
Toothpick • Eye Pin • Paintbrush • Varnish

These yummy cupcakes are perfect for Valentine's Day,
but they're great any old day of the week.

Instructions:

1. Create a muffin-like shape with red clay.

2. Make small circular motions with a needle tool (or toothpick) for the sides of the cake. This will create a crumby, cake texture.

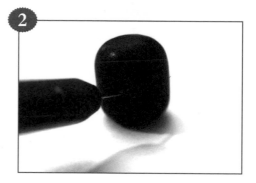

3. Repeat step 2 at the top of the cake, to look like it's been bitten.

4. Mix white solid clay and liquid clay to create the frosting. Add this on the bitten area.

5. Insert an eye pin.

6. Bake using the instructions on your clay package.

7. Let the charm cool completely before glazing the top for a glossy shine.

HEDGEHOG

Did you know some people keep hedgehogs as pets?
Get your very own with these little hedgehog charms.

Instructions:

1. Start with a ball of brown clay. This will be the body of the hedgehog.

2. Add ecru-clay colored for the head. Pinch the clay to form a pointed shape.

3. Add black clay for the eyes and nose.

4. Add the ears. Indent them with a dotting tool.

5.   Use pink clay for the blush.

6.   Use a needle tool or toothpick to indent the body for its quills.

7.   Insert an eye pin.

8.   Bake using the instructions on your clay package.

9.   Glaze the charm with varnish to give your hedgehog a glossy shine.

POLAR BEAR

Difficulty Level: **Easy**

Materials:

Polymer Clay (White) • Toothpick • Acrylic Paint (Black, Pink)

Brrr! It's cold in the arctic, but you'll keep warm with your polar bear bud by your side.

Instructions:

1. Start with a ball of white clay.

2. Pinch the top corner for its snout.

3. Add little white spheres for the ears.

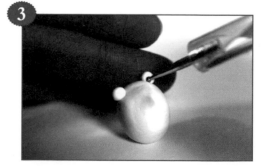

4. Indent the ears with a dotting tool.

5. Insert an eye pin.

6. Bake using the instructions on your clay package.

7. After the charm has cooled completely, paint the facial features. Use a toothpick dipped in black acrylic paint to draw on the eyes and nose.

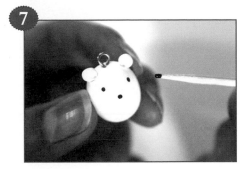

8. Use pink acrylic paint for the blush.

9. Let the paint dry completely.

10. Glaze the charm with varnish to set the paint and give your bear a glossy shine.

CHOCOLATE-DIPPED STRAWBERRY

Difficulty Level: **Easy**

Materials:

Polymer Clay (Red, Brown, Green, White) • Rolling Pin •
Blade • Dotting Tool • Eye Pin • Paintbrush • Varnish

Sweet berries are made even better with a little chocolate. Make as many as you want for a platter of them.

Instructions:

1. Start with red clay and pinch one side for the strawberry's shape.

2. Flatten a sheet of green clay.

3. Cut out a star-like, pointed shape with a blade. Be careful! These will be the leaves of the strawberry.

4. Add the leaves to the red clay.

5. Use a dotting tool to indent the strawberry.

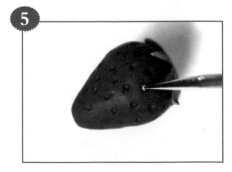

6. Cover the lower portion of the strawberry with a sheet of brown clay.

7. Add a strand of white clay in a zigzag pattern.

8. Insert an eye pin.

9. Bake using the instructions on your clay package.

10. Let the charm cool completely before glazing with varnish.

RAINBOW CAKE

Difficulty Level: **Medium**

Materials:

Polymer Clay (Red, Orange, Yellow, Green, Blue, Purple, White) • Rolling Pin • Circular Cookie Cutter • Blade • Needle Tool or Toothpick • Liquid Clay • Eye Pin • Paintbrush • Varnish

Taste the rainbow with this multi-colored cake. You'll never have to choose a favorite color with this rainbow charm cake.

Instructions:

1. Flatten a sheet of red clay.

2. Cut out a circle with a cookie cutter.

3. Repeat steps 1 and 2 with all the other colors of the rainbow, as well as five white circles.

4. Stack the portions, making sure to separate the colors with white circles.

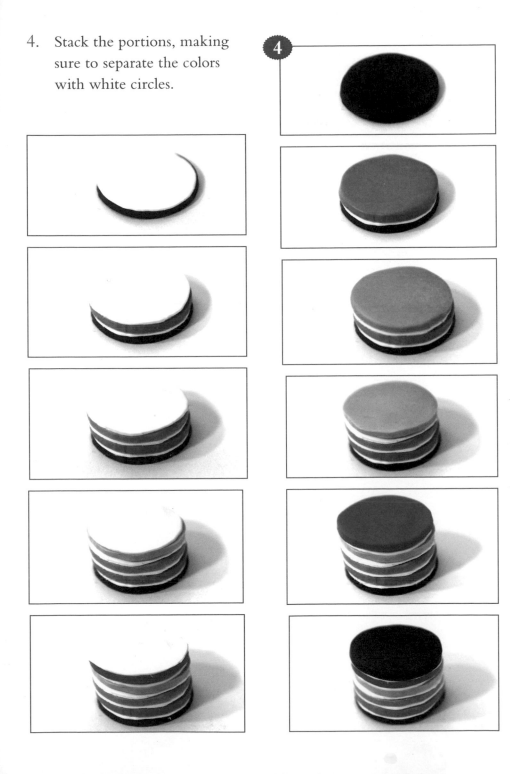

5. With a blade, cut out a slice of cake. TIP: Leave your cake in the freezer for five minutes so it's easier to cut.

6. Use a needle tool (or toothpick) to texture the cake. Move the needle in circular motions.

7. Mix solid white clay and liquid clay for the frosting. Spread the mixture onto the cake.

8. Insert an eye pin.

9. Bake using the instructions on your clay package.

10. Let the charm cool completely before glazing the frosting with varnish for a glossy shine.

PiZZA

Eata'pizza, eata'pizza! Grab a slice with this cheese-
covered charm. *Bon appetito!*

Instructions:

1. Flatten a circular sheet of ecru-colored clay.

2. Fold over the edges.

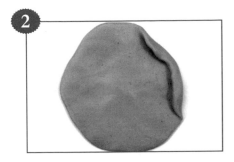

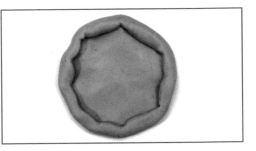

3. Texture the crust with the bristles of a toothbrush.

4. Dust the crust with orange chalk pastels. This will give it a baked look.

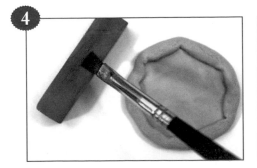

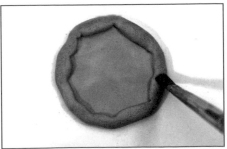

5. Add thin pieces of yellow clay.

6. Use a dotting tool to texture the yellow clay.

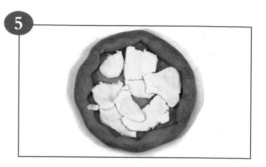

7. Mix liquid clay and red chalk pastels for the pizza sauce.

8. Using your fingers, gently apply the mixture to the cheese.

9. Dust the cheese with brown chalk pastels to give it a baked effect.

10. Add the toppings. Mix brown and red clay for the pepperonis. Texture them with a dotting tool.

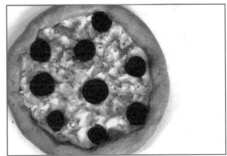

11. Add thin, green slices for the peppers.

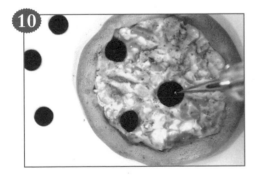

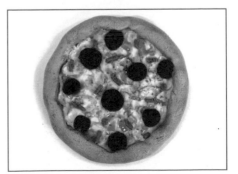

12. Use black clay for the olives.

13. Cut out a slice of pizza with a blade.

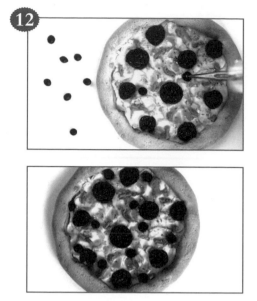

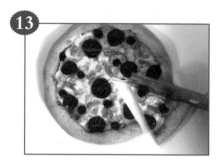

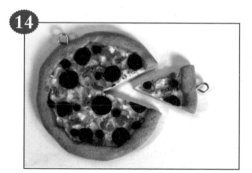

14. Insert an eye pin.

15. Bake using the instructions on your clay package.

16. Let the pizza cool completely. Apply varnish to the cheese to give it a glossy shine.

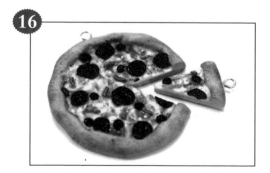

MACARON

Difficulty Level: **Easy**

Materials:

Polymer Clay (Pink, Red, Translucent) • Needle Tool or
Toothpick • Eye Pin • Paintbrush • Varnish

You don't have to visit the Eiffel Tower for a taste of
Paris. Swap your plane ticket for this sweet macaron
charm instead. *Oui, oui!*

Instructions:

1. Flatten a ball of pink clay into a dome shape.

2. Texture the bottom edge of the dome using a needle tool or toothpick. Make circular motions to create a crumbly texture.

3. Create a second dome.

4. Mix red and translucent clay. Form a flat circular shape.

5. Place the red clay between the two domes.

6. Insert an eye pin.

7. Bake using the instructions on your clay package.

8. Let the charm cool completely before glazing the filling with varnish for a glossy shine.

HOT DOG

Nothing's better on a summer day than a glass of
lemonade and a hot dog with all the trimmings. Which
toppings will you choose for your clay charm dog?

Instructions:

1. Create an ecru-colored clay log.

2. With a blade, cut halfway into the center of the log.

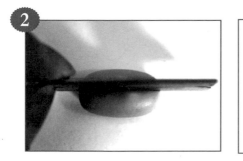

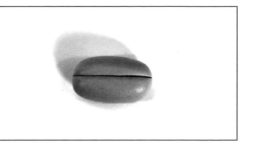

3. Slightly pull the two halves apart.

4. Mix red and brown clay for the hot dog. Add the hot dog to the center of the bun.

5. Texture the bun with the bristles of a toothbrush.

6. Dust the sides of the bun with orange and brown chalk pastels to give it a baked look.

7. Add the mustard with a thin strand of yellow clay.

8. Insert an eye pin.

9. Bake using the instructions on your clay package.

10. Let the charm cool completely before glazing the hot dog and mustard with varnish for a glossy shine.